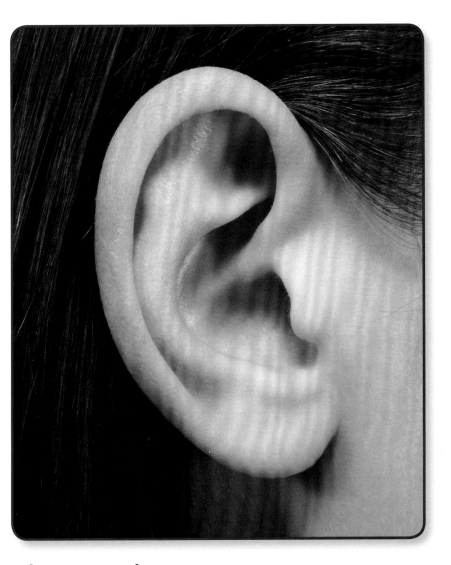

I hear with my ears!

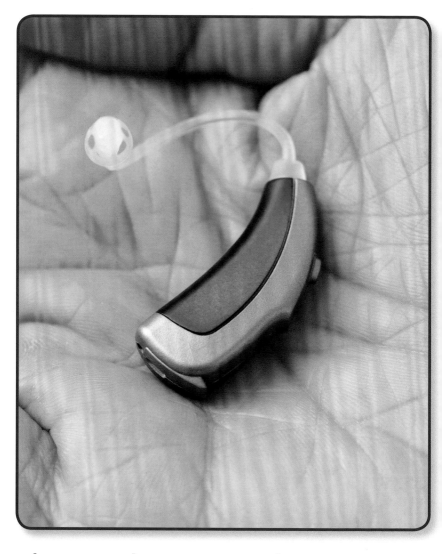

I have a hearing aid.
I got it a year ago.

I Hear with My Ears

Practicing the EER Sound

Novak Popovic

Rosen
PHONICS
READERS

Rosen
Classroom™

How do I hear?

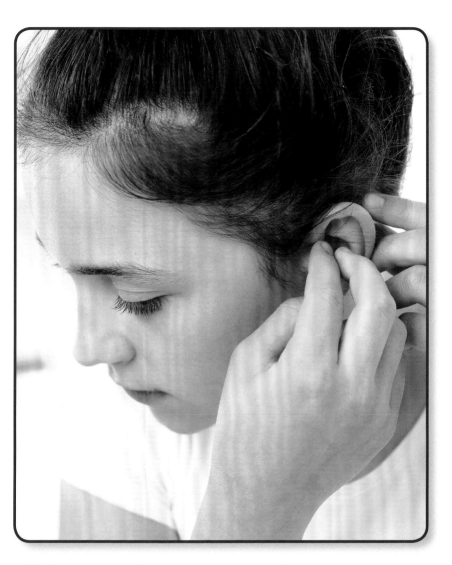

I like my hearing aid.
It helps my ears hear.

I hear a deer with my ears.
The deer hears me, too.

I hear a horse nearby.
The horse hears me, too.

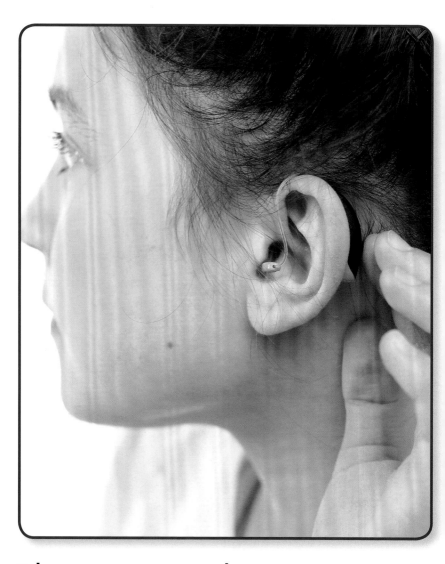

I hear music with my ears.

I hear music loud and clear.

Music always cheers me up!

I love to hear everything
near me.

What can you hear
with your ears?